THE SINGLE MARKET

CONTENTS

Across Europe, millions of citizens and thousands of companies, big and small, benefit from the European single market. The removal of frontiers inside the European Union in 1993 is now a fact of life. Companies have entered new markets, have struck up transnational partnerships, have restructured production to exploit the opportunities of a home market of 370 million. Ordinary folk have benefited in two ways. On the one hand, they have extra freedom and mobility to shop, work or live in another EU country than their own. As consumers (and without having to move), they profit from the increased choice of goods and services as well as from the keener prices that the single market has brought them. Despite its achievements, work is needed to complete and to consolidate the single market. While goods, services and capital now move freely, people are still subject to identity checks at some internal borders. The problem here is to reconcile personal mobility with the need to control international crime and curb illegal immigration. At the business level, partnerships between the European Commission in Brussels and national governments are needed to ensure that single market rules are applied correctly (which is not always the case) and that new national regulations do not raise *de facto* new barriers to trade. The creation of the single market was the beginning of a process not the end. Managing and improving this enterprise is an ongoing challenge.

A positive balance sheet

The creation of the European single market is probably the greatest project of economic integration ever undertaken. Within seven years, the European Union (or European Community as it was then) and its Member States transformed 12 separate national markets into one unit. This huge task, begun in 1985, was largely completed by 1 January 1993. Since then its benefits have been extended to the three new EU countries which joined at the beginning of 1995.

The achievements of the single market must be consolidated and developed. The scope of this task should not be underestimated. The single market is the essential foundation for the next phase of EU integration, the move to economic and monetary union (EMU), and provides an essential underpinning for Europe's economic growth and competitiveness.

Despite its aim of integrating national economies, the single market does not seek to eliminate national differences in language, culture, identity or tradition. On the contrary, it is based on the recognition by member countries of each other's national regulations. It also recognizes the principle of subsidiarity, where decisions are taken at the closest possible level to the citizen.

The creation of the single market was a complex process involving the adoption of detailed legislation in a wide range of policy areas which was needed to get rid of physical, technical and fiscal barriers.

Personal mobility

For ordinary travellers, frontier controls within the single market have been considerably reduced. Customs checks have been eliminated altogether and long waits at land border crossings, which could last for hours at busy times, are a thing of the past. Identity checks still remain, especially at sea and airports although the aim is to eliminate these too.

The removal of frontier controls was accompanied by the lifting of restrictions on the amount of goods travellers could buy in another EU country and bring home with them, provided their purchases are for personal consumption. They can take home a carload of goods of all sorts: food and drink, consumer electronics, household appliances, computers, antiques and so on.

The taxes on such goods are paid in the normal way in the country where they are bought. Travellers gain most, therefore on items where there are significant price or tax differences from one country to another. This is often the case for tobacco, alcohol and fuel. As a result, they may be asked to justify that goods are indeed for personal consumption when certain indicative limits are exceeded. These are 800 cigarettes, 90 litres of wine, 110 litres of beer or 10 litres of spirits.

However, people shopping around for the lowest priced new cars must pay value-added tax (VAT) in the country where the car is to be registered rather than where it was bought. This means that the buyer can benefit from lower vehicle prices, which can vary by up to 30% from one country to another, but not from a tax regime which may be more favourable than that of his home country.

In addition to their tax-free shopping, travellers can still benefit from duty-free purchases when travelling by air and sea between Member States, although such concessions should, strictly speaking, no longer exist within a single market. They will remain in force until 1999 and special limits will continue to apply on duty-free allowances until then.

Choice of residence and place of work

But the single market is much more than travel and bargain-hunting. One of the fundamental principles is that workers, self-employed people and trainees are free to take jobs and live in another Member State. Unemployed people are also free to look for work in another Member State without losing their rights to social security.

This right of residence has been progressively extended to include other non-economically active categories who can show that they have sickness insurance and the means to support themselves, such as students, pensioners and persons of independent resources who are not part of the workforce. It is now possible, therefore, for pensioners from northern Europe to retire to the Mediterranean sunbelt provided they have enough income from their home country, or other sources, to make sure they do not become a financial burden on the host country.

The single market has also put in place a series of directives to give workers a certain level of social protection. In doing so, the EU has been particularly concerned to level upwards — raising the level of standards in those countries where they were lowest.

EKA

Health and safety in the workplace is one area where the social aspects of the single market have made most progress. A general directive was implemented at the beginning of 1993 fixing a set of principles for worker safety and protection. More specific directives have been adopted concerning working hours, the use of equipment and the wearing of protective clothing.

There has been tremendous progress in freedom of movement within the Union, but identity papers are still checked at some airports, partly because the governments of the Member States are keen to see that free movement does not benefit international terrorism, illegal immigration and the drugs trade. Measures will be taken to deal effectively with these scourges of our times through permanent intensive co-operation between the forces of law and order in all the Member States.

All EU members, except the United Kingdom, adopted the Social Charter of basic workers' rights in 1989 and subscribed to the Social Chapter of the Maastricht Treaty on European Union. In this framework they adopted, in 1994, a Directive which provides for the creation of works councils in transnational firms in Europe. In these councils, workers will be informed and consulted on issues affecting their future.

A landmark decision

EU ministers for social affairs formally adopted the works councils Directive on 22 September 1994 after several years of negotiations. Under the Directive, transnational companies with 1 000 or more employees in Europe and at least 150 in two or more Member States will have to create a mechanism for informing and consulting their workforce.

The Directive will apply to about 1 200 multinational firms (of European and non-European origin) employing about 4 million workers across the Union.

Governments were given two years to September 1996 to transpose the Directive into national law. Until then, management and labour from any company affected by the Directive could negotiate their own voluntary agreement for worker consultation. A number of international firms have done so.

After the deadline, companies will have to introduce worker consultation mechanisms which comply with the format set out in the Directive. The first of these 'compulsory' agreements will take effect in 1999.

Not all aspects of social and labour laws have been incorporated into the single market. National governments, and not the European Union, are responsible for laws concerning the hiring and firing of workers and for trade union legislation.

The general right of nationals of one country to live in another is now enshrined in the Treaty on European Union in the chapter relating to citizenship of the Union. In addition, the Treaty gives such residents the right to vote or stand as a candidate in local or European elections under the same conditions as nationals of their country of residence.

The freedom to travel or to go about one's business throughout Europe as easily as in one's own country is for the citizen the most potent symbol of the single market and of the European Union itself.

What is the Social Charter?

The Social Charter or 'Community Charter of the Fundamental Social Rights of Workers' is a solemn declaration adopted by the Heads of State or Government of 11 Member States of the European Community (the 12 Member States less the United Kingdom) at the Strasbourg European Council in December 1989.

It is based on the great principles underlying the European model of labour law and proclaims rights in the following fields:
- freedom of movement,
- employment and remuneration,
- improvement of living and working conditions,
- social protection,
- freedom of association and collective bargaining,
- vocational training,
- equal treatment for men and women,
- information, consultation and participation of workers,
- health protection and safety at the workplace,
- protection of children and adolescents,
- the rights of elderly persons,
- the rights of disabled people.

More competitive companies

The single market helps make European firms more competitive by creating the largest market in the industrialized world. The aim is to provide them with the opportunity for bigger production runs and economies of scale as well as simplified standards and access to contracts awarded by public authorities in other EU countries.

This will enable them to cut costs, lowering prices for the European consumer. In addition, they will also be more able to compete effectively in global markets with their American and Japanese rivals who already enjoy the benefits of large integrated home markets.

They have also been able to cut costs in other ways. The removal of frontier controls for road transportation has, for instance, reduced the average time it takes a truck to cross Europe by two days. One international express delivery company says the open highways created by the single market have cut its global operating costs by 15%. Other transport firms also quote savings, but at a lower level.

A simple framework for transnational cooperation

Since July 1989, EU firms have had at their disposal a new legal tool for transnational cooperation enabling them to engage in joint activities such as research and development, purchase, production and sale in the widest possible variety of fields. The status of European Economic Interest Grouping (EEIG) helps them to become more competitive by spreading costs or risks or using joint services with partners from other Member States. However, the purpose of the EEIG is not to enable firms to make individual gains. Governed by EU law, the EEIG enjoys full legal recognition.

Thanks to the single market, companies can sell goods and offer services in any country of the Union just as easily as if they were trading on their domestic market.

Capital restrictions have been lifted enabling banks, companies and individuals to invest their money in the currency and market of their choice. At the same time, banks, insurance

EKA

If there is to be a genuine single market with real growth and job creation potential, a European communications network is a must. Europe's various countries and regions are to be merged into a dynamic entity through the trans-European networks of arterial communications carrying the European Union's economic life-blood. All modes of transport (by road, rail, air and inland waterway) are to be covered, as are telecommunications and energy.

Too much harmonization in the European Union?

Under the subsidiarity principle, the European Union legislates only where action is more effective at Union level than at national level. The European Commission and the Member States ensure that the principle is observed.

Most harmonization measures are requested by governments and firms to ensure that the single market works correctly without any distortions of competition.

The European Union has established the principle of mutual recognition. Any product manufactured in a Member State can be marketed in all Union countries on condition that the aims of national regulations, for example in matters of safety, are not undermined.

companies and investment firms can now operate throughout the European Union from their home territory on the basis of European passports issued by their national regulatory authority. Previously they could only operate in countries outside their national territory if they set up a subsidiary company there subject to local regulation.

In general terms, the single market consolidated the principle of mutual recognition of national rules and regulations instead of creating a whole new series of Euro-norms and standards. The principle is that Member States have agreed to accept each other's existing rules and standards as being equivalent to their own.

Mutual recognition is not only helping banks and insurance companies to serve customers throughout the EU efficiently and at competitive prices. It also enables goods, from electronic equipment to foodstuffs, to be traded unhampered across national borders. Individual companies can now sell their goods in other EU Member States based on a single standard – that of their home country.

Moreover, the fact that each Member State accepts the others' educational qualifications as being roughly equivalent has enhanced the mobility among the liberal professions and workers with specific job skills. This mobility is regarded as a valuable asset for a truly competitive European economy.

Big companies were quick to identify the advantages to be derived from the single market. They were among the earliest supporters of the Commission's 1992 programme first set out in a landmark White Paper of 1985. They gave the project strong support throughout. They also took timely action to organize their production, marketing and financial structures so as to take early advantage of the disappearance of frontiers.

In order to enable small and medium-sized enterprises (SMEs) to draw maximum benefit from the single market, the European Commission has taken a number of initiatives, including the creation of the network of Euro-Info Centres. These centres, there are 210 throughout the EU, provide access to information and advice to SMEs.

Reactions are positive

The abolition of internal EU frontiers is already having a positive impact on the way small and medium-sized enterprises (SMEs) do business. This emerges clearly from a survey carried out by the European Commission through its Euro-Info Centres (EICs).

Virtually all companies participating in the survey said the removal of frontier controls had speeded up the delivery of goods and cut transport costs considerably. In some cases, the increased competition among transport firms had enabled manufacturing companies to save up to 50% on delivery costs.

Yes to the single market

More than half of Europeans (54%) feel 'very/rather hopeful' following the establishment of the single European market on 1 January 1993. Some 35% feel 'very/rather fearful' and 11% have no opinion. The most optimistic are the Dutch (70% 'very/rather hopeful'), the Irish (69%), the Greeks (64%), the Luxembourgers (62%) and the Danes (61%). They are followed by the Italians and Belgians (57%), the Portuguese (54%), the Spaniards and the British (53%), the Germans (51%) and the French (47%).

These figures are the result of an opinion poll taken in the 12 Member States of the European Union in the spring of 1994.

The Single Market — Hope or fear?

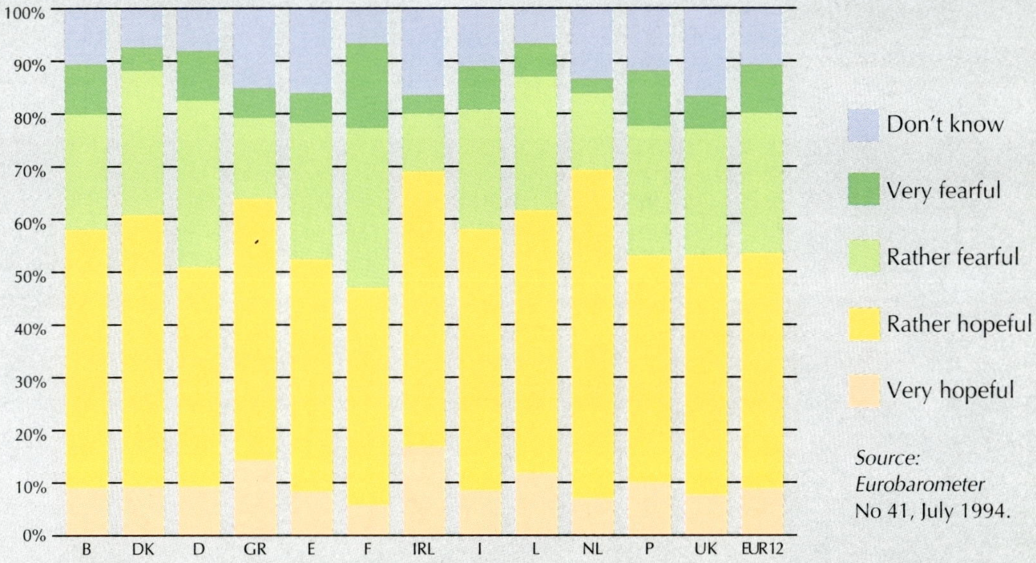

Source: Eurobarometer No 41, July 1994.

Cooperation between firms

The European Union has created various tools for firms seeking a partnership, such as:

The Europartnership Programme, which, twice a year, organizes direct encounter meetings between heads of firms. Its purpose is to encourage cooperation and to promote business agreements between small and medium-sized enterprises (SMEs) in regions whose development is lagging behind or which are undergoing industrial reconversion and those of other countries in Europe and the Mediterranean area.

The Business Cooperation Network (BC-Net), which is an instrument available to SMEs wishing to engage in a confidential search for partners. Using an extended computerized network the system is able to compare the profiles of firms' requests submitted through the intermediary of 600 business consultants.

The BCC (Business Cooperation Centre) Network, whose purpose is to promote financial, commercial and technical cooperation between firms. It operates through the exchange of non-confidential documents setting out requests for cooperation.

For additional information, firms can contact their regional Euro-Info Centre.

Many had developed new forms of cooperation with partners in other EU countries in order to enter new markets. They include subcontracting, licensing, distribution or agency agreements. A Belgian firm producing specialized insulation systems for the building sector increased its exports from zero to 60% of its output after signing up a foreign partner. Similarly, a British cartography and survey company raised exports to nearly 50% from practically nil thanks to a cooperation agreement with a German firm.

To compete in new markets successful firms have had to develop new products or improve existing ones. A number of respondents said the new export mentality and know-how they had acquired in the European single market had encouraged them to enter overseas markets as well.

The picture is mixed when it comes to the acceptance by EU countries of each other's standards and type-approval procedures or to fair competition in bidding for public contracts. This is not surprising. These are areas where experience needs to be built up over a period of time before definitive conclusions can be drawn. But the correct implementation and operation of single market rules in these sensitive areas will require close and regular monitoring.

In the main, companies surveyed had positive experience of the mutual recognition procedures for tests and type-approval procedures both in terms of increased exports and in the reduction of costs for type-approval and certification. A Belgian manufacturer of earth-moving equipment said its bill for type-approval procedures had been cut by 50%. However, a number of firms said that in their view mutual recognition procedures simply had not worked.

The survey was based on a limited sample of companies in nine EU Member States. The European Commission is preparing a comprehensive analysis of the economic impact and benefits of the single market to be published in 1996.

EKA

Special rules have been put in place regarding carriage of arms, explosives, artworks, radioactive substances, drugs and waste, to avoid the single market turning out to be a criminals' paradise.

Regional cooperation

The LACE programme (linkage, assistance and cooperation for the European border regions), which came into existence in 1990, is the latest outcome of the deliberations of the Association of European Border Regions.

The programme, which is open to all Europe's border regions, concerns first and foremost exchanges of experience and information on the regions. It covers a number of fields — technical assistance (provision of premises and equipment), the promotion of a network of border areas (which may result in joint market research or group purchases) and dissemination and publicity activities (joint marketing and promotion strategies between enterprises in border regions). A data bank serves to complete this arrangement.

Striking a regional balance

To ensure that the benefits of the single market are distributed fairly and equitably among all regions and all citizens, the Union has introduced an important series of parallel actions and policies. These include greatly increased financial support for poorer member countries and regions from the EU's Structural Funds and the creation of trans-European networks (TENs) for telecommunications, transport and energy distribution so as to link national networks in an integrated European structure.

The Single European Act (SEA) of 1987, which provided the route map for the creation of the single market, reinforced the notion of social and economic cohesion between the rich and poor regions of the EU. The aim was for the richer countries to help the poorer ones accelerate their economic development so that they, too, can enjoy the full benefits of the single market.

This principle was enshrined in the Cohesion Fund, which was set up under the Maastricht Treaty to foster growth in the four poorest countries — Greece, Portugal, Spain and Ireland. It builds on the solidarity already created within the EU by the European Regional Development Fund (ERDF) and the Social Fund.

The primary concern is to raise the level of economic development in the cohesion countries so that, when the time comes, they can participate alongside other Member States in the final phase of economic and monetary union and the introduction of a single currency, the euro.

Safeguarding the single market's success

Although they took 35 years to realize, the goals of the single market are enshrined in the European Union's founding Treaty of Rome which became the constitution for the future European Union in 1958. There we find already the list of the single market's four freedoms: the free movement of goods, services, capital and people.

While tariffs on goods had disappeared from intra-EU trade in the 1960s, no concerted action had been taken to remove non-tariff barriers and other obstacles, which kept national markets fragmented, blocking the creation of an integrated single market. This changed when Jacques Delors became president of the European Commission in 1985. The achievement of a frontier-free single market became his first priority.

By the end-1992 deadline, the main body of single market rules was in place. All but a few of the nearly 300 items of legislation had been adopted on schedule. Responsibility for the actual running of the single market since January 1995 has been in the hands of Mario Monti, the member of the European Commission in charge of the internal market, financial services, customs and taxation.

EKA

EKA

Free movement of capital is now a reality in the single market. Union citizens are free to conduct their banking business in all the Union Member States. Greece alone enjoys a transitional period for short-term operations. The problem of inter-State bank transfers, however, has still not been solved properly. Transfers take much longer and cost more than transfers within a given country. But the position is expected to improve in 1996.

Easy crossing of borders

Checks on goods at the Union's internal borders came to an end on 1 January 1993. Customs officers, tax inspectors and veterinary inspectors have disappeared from internal border posts. Random identity checks are still carried out at some border crossings until such time as free movement of persons has been fully established.

Travellers no longer have to undergo checks on the goods they are transporting and lorries can now cross borders with ease, sparing them the long periods they used to spend waiting, for example, at the customs posts at the Mont Blanc tunnel, the Channel ports or other border crossings. The 30 or so documents which the lorry driver used to have to produce when crossing a Community border have now been compressed into one — the Single Administrative Document (SAD).

Now for the hard part

It has long been recognized that despite its complexity, setting up the single market would be a relatively easy task compared with actually running it. The management task has been made more difficult by the fact that the first year of the single market, 1993, coincided with the low point of one of the worst recessions the EU has known.

Post-recession, the single market must be consolidated as the foundation on which a series of EU initiatives contained in the December 1993 White Paper on growth, competitiveness and employment are to be based. The single market itself cannot act as an economic motor to boost growth and create jobs. But it can act as a catalyst in the strategy for economic expansion of the EU and its member governments. A smooth-functioning single market will respond rapidly and efficiently to measures taken at Union and national level to stimulate growth. It presents a much more credible platform for economic growth for the EU than would have been possible even a few years ago.

But the ultimate success of the single market will depend on constructive cooperation between the EU and Member States to ensure that rules are fairly and correctly applied and that the inevitable new problems that arise are dealt with swiftly and effectively.

Now that it is in place, the single market has developed a dynamism of its own. New needs will arise requiring

Does the single market serve everyone's interests?

The single market will help to increase competition. As a result, the final consumer will gradually be offered a wider choice of products at more attractive prices.

In the single market consumers can engage in remote purchasing from other Member States without having to worry about VAT when the goods enter their own country. Responsibility for calculating, declaring and paying VAT now lies with the seller, regardless of the place of taxation.

In addition, goods received as gifts or acquired by way of marriage or inheritance can move freely within the Union and do not have to be declared for VAT purposes.

new policies to be developed or existing ones modified. It is already clear that further advances need to be made in improving the conditions in which business operates. The extension of consumers' rights, the acceleration of information flows and the development of trans-European networks have been identified as other priorities.

Identifying problems

In a number of areas, the single market is incomplete. In others, EU legislation is being applied differently from one Member State to another, thereby creating *de facto* trade barriers. The result is uncertainty, which makes firms, particularly SMEs, hesitate and hold back rather than push ahead to exploit the full advantages of the single market.

The biggest problems have arisen in the area of mutual recognition of national norms and standards in those sectors where there is no European legislation for harmonizing national rules. A number of Member States are still finding reasons or pretexts to refuse the import of goods from other EU countries on grounds linked to national regulations concerning norms or standards.

The European Commission has received hundreds of complaints about such illegal barriers. They concern such widely diverse items as caravans, pharmaceuticals, Greek ceramic tiles, Belgian bedding quilts and even Dutch radishes.

The Commission and the European Parliament are concerned that unless this and other related problems can be solved rapidly the credibility of much of the single market programme may be permanently damaged. The Commission has adopted a strategic programme in a bid to keep the single market firmly on track.

EKA

Consumers can now buy what they want where they want in the single market without having to pay duty on the way home.

Mobility for national officials

Communication through computers is very effective. But, while working together on the ground may, on the face of it, seem rather less straightforward, it is equally important. The Union's Mattaeus programme, launched by the Commission in 1991, is designed to help customs officers to become more familiar with each other. This exchange and training programme entails training courses, intensive language courses at the various national customs training schools, training seminars and, above all, exchanges of national officials from different Member States. The purpose is to encourage mobility among civil servants, which is an essential requirement for the proper application of EU legislation in the Member States of the Union. In October 1992, the European Commission also launched Karolus, which is a programme of exchanges between officials whose duties entail the application of the rules governing the single market. Of two months' duration, exchanges are intended to encourage harmonized interpretation and application of the new European Union rules concerning the single market.

EKA

Long queues of lorries at frontiers are a thing of the past, and the haulage industry is glad of that. The savings on overheads the free movement has helped the Union's businesses make, are estimated at several billion ecus. The disappearance of customs forms has made life much easier for all the firms concerned.

Free movement of persons

The biggest piece of unfinished business in the original single market programme is that of the free movement of persons. The EU and the Member States are committed to removing all frontier controls on persons crossing from one EU country to another. The level of identity checks has already been reduced, but they are proving hard to abolish.

Member States are unwilling to accept open frontiers and mobility if the price they have to pay is more mobile criminals and less security, and unchecked immigration.

To provide the citizen with full freedom of movement and in parallel ensure his or her security and protection, a number of actions are necessary. Governments have had to devise ways of working, individually and together, to combat illegal immigration and maintain effective action against criminals, if necessary by spot checks away from national frontiers.

Freedom of movement within the EU implies that the removal of internal frontier controls is matched by a reinforcement of controls at the external frontiers of the Union. With the disappearance of internal frontiers, people from other countries, once inside the territory of the Union, can move about as freely as local citizens. This means that Member States must be able to rely on each other to carry out effective and harmonized controls at the points of entry.

Will open frontiers make drug-trafficking easier?

Seizures of drugs and the arrest of traffickers have not taken place at the Union's internal borders for some years now.

Control of cross-border traffic in drugs is now carried out to greater effect at the external borders, even though they include 10 000 km of coastline, and at sensitive points of entry such as international ports and airports.

A system of close cooperation between the police forces and judicial authorities of the Member States has been established to reinforce controls.

The way ahead

Ten of the EU countries are moving ahead progressively in their efforts to enable controls at their common frontiers to disappear. This initiative of the so-called Schengen group (Germany, France, the Benelux countries, Italy, Spain, Austria, Portugal and Greece) has led to the adoption of some far-reaching regulations providing for a common system of issuing visas and a common list of countries whose nationals require a visa to enter any of the Schengen countries. The Schengen group takes its name from the small Luxembourg town where five of the ten signed an agreement in 1985 to remove internal frontiers between them.

As part of the Schengen Agreement, police forces will assist each other in detecting and preventing crime. They will be assisted by a computerized information and communications system (the Schengen information system or SIS). National police forces will have the right to pursue fleeing criminals and drug traffickers onto the territory of a neighbouring Schengen State.

The Schengen Convention took effect during 1995 for most participants. France is temporarily applying an exception clause to its borders with Belgium and Luxembourg. The Schengen countries hope the other EU members will adopt the same principles at a later stage.

In the meantime, the entry into force of the Treaty on European Union in November 1993 enabled the EU to accelerate its own work to consolidate the freedom of movement of persons. The new provisions for cooperation in justice and home affairs will help to underpin personal mobility by increasing the efficiency of action at national and EU level to stop illegal immigration and to improve the fight against terrorism, drug running and other forms of international crime.

The European Union — An 'easy target'?

The Community rules governing the operation of the internal market comprise measures to combat fraud and counterfeiting.

The information exchange schemes set up between national customs authorities enable the Member States to cooperate effectively on combating fraud and trafficking, whether of an economic nature (false declarations concerning the origin of goods) or connected with the illicit transport of protected species of plants or animals, drugs or prohibited goods. In January 1993, a computerized network was set up to monitor compliance with the rules on meat and animals at the Union's borders.

A computerized network is planned to link up the frontier inspection posts responsible for conducting veterinary checks so as to prevent fraud in connection with live animals and animal products.

As regards efforts to combat counterfeiting, the Member States apply the same customs rules at the Union's external borders. According to these rules, any firm has the right to have the customs impound counterfeit products which damage its interests.

The European Commission has submitted proposals for certain visa policy measures and a revised draft of its External Frontiers Convention. These provide for the reciprocal recognition of national visas, meaning that a third-country national will require only one visa to visit any number of EU States.

Keeping goods on the move

The removal of barriers to the free movement of goods was possibly the most dramatic achievement of the single market programme. It is also the area where achievements appear to be most at risk. For instance, while firms across Europe acknowledge that they have benefited from the removal of border controls, some may feel this advantage may be partly offset by the extra paperwork they now have to carry out themselves.

According to a survey of British firms carried out by the Confederation of British Industries (CBI), this is particularly true in the area of value-added tax (VAT) collection. The movement of goods has been speeded up as a result of the decision to put an end to the system of checking on VAT payments on exported goods at frontier crossing points. Companies themselves must instead submit documentation to their own national VAT authorities.

In the same way, trade statistics which were formerly collected at frontiers by customs officials must now be provided on the basis of regular returns directly by firms. However, the practical administrative impact on firms of these requirements can vary from one EU country to another.

New deal for VAT in 1997

The present VAT system is a compromise and an interim arrangement. Although it does away with controls at frontiers, the system still requires VAT on a traded item to be paid in the country where it is imported.

Thus, the importer pays VAT to his government rather than to the firm selling the goods to him (the exporter) which would be normal procedure within a single market structure. EU governments opted for a transitional arrangement to give them time to prepare for the full adaptation of the VAT payment and collection system to the single market. The definitive VAT system, where tax would be paid in the country of production of an item rather than its country of consumption, is due to be introduced in 1997.

Although the free movement of goods is now a reality, some exporting firms (particularly SMEs) have encountered difficulties in having product standards accepted by the national authorities in importing countries. They may also experience discrimination when bidding for government and other public contracts in EU countries other than their own.

Monthly payment of VAT by firms

What has not changed:

As a rule, VAT remains payable in the country for which goods are destined.

What has changed:

Goods now cross borders without undergoing checks.
The removal of the borders means that VAT is no longer paid to customs at the time of importation. Intra-Community VAT is now declared and paid to the tax authorities in the same way as internal VAT. Furthermore, every month firms have to submit to the customs a declaration of transactions in goods between Member States, which is used to draw up statistics on external trade and enable the national administrative bodies to survey intra-Community operations.

EKA

EKA

In the single market quality controls are run on the basis of mutual recognition. Each Member State trusts the controls and certification of the others. And the system has been found to work. National diversities, customs and traditions are preserved, and the range of goods available for the consumer to choose from is expanded.

Standards are a particularly sensitive issue. Technical regulations are required to make sure that goods are safe and that they work properly. But these have traditionally varied considerably from one Member State to another. What started out as legitimate rules setting product standards, safety norms, health and even security requirements had become in some instances instruments of trade protectionism.

Items such as cars and television sets had to be modified, sometimes in innumerable small ways, to meet different national requirements. As a result, exporters were penalized twice. They had to produce modified products for each market, forgoing the scale economies involved in producing one model for all markets. In addition, they had to pay extra costs to have their products type-approved by the authorities in each importing country.

Small countries which set special national standards to protect their own companies from outside competition have come to realize the shortsightedness of this approach. Their domestic markets turn out to be too small to enable home companies to survive. These firms then have to change product specifications anyway if they wish to export to their bigger neighbours. In this way, national standards are not a protective defence against imports but an obstacle to local exports.

EKA

Food legislation in the Union Member States has evolved in very different ways over the decades. Experts agreed that Community legislation was generally far too detailed as regards jams, sugar and fruit juices, for instance. They are now working on proposals for much simpler legislation that will cover only the main principles, leaving national and regional customs and traditions to regulate the rest. The consumer should be the prime beneficiary.

The single market sought to eliminate these problems by getting Member States to accept each other's standards as being equivalent in most instances. Where the creation of harmonized European standards remained necessary, these were to be kept to a minimum.

Harmonization of standards was recognized as indispensable in at least two cases:

1. Where there are differences in national legislation concerning essential requirements such as public health, technical security or consumer protection;

2. When harmonized rules and standardized products are necessary for industry to achieve economies of scale in a specific product market.

But to avoid over-regulation, a new approach to harmonization was devised. It stipulated that EU legislators should limit themselves to defining the essential objectives and requirements and should delegate technical aspects to outside standardization bodies, preferably at European level.

It is estimated that about 20 to 30% of goods traded across EU frontiers are the object of harmonized standards. The rest are governed by mutual recognition procedures. Increasing use is also made of procedures whereby firms can attest to the conformity of their own goods via a system of self-certification.

However, there is considerable evidence that differences in the way the new rules are being interpreted at national level is causing considerable difficulties for firms expecting to make use of liberalized access to their competitors' markets.

Services catch up

The services sector is the biggest employer in all EU countries, accounting for 60% of jobs in the Union. It contributes 62% to the gross domestic product (GDP) of the EU, compared with 35% from manufacturing industry and 3% from agriculture.

Despite the sector's importance, the freedom for companies to provide services throughout the EU got off to a slow start. In financial services, for example, only banking services were fully liberalized by the single market deadline of 1 January 1993. The single market in insurance services came into being on 1 July 1994. The corresponding directive covering the liberalization of investment services took effect on 1 January 1996.

In spring 1994, an EU directive was adopted to guarantee savers and investors a minimum level of protection in cases of international bankruptcies like the spectacular case of the Bank of Credit and Commerce International (BCCI) where thousands of small savers in Europe lost money. In such cases they will receive a guaranteed indemnity of up to ECU 20 000.

On the basis of EU legislation, firms offering banking and financial services are able to do so via the single passport (or operating licence) issued by the regulatory authority in their home country. This removes the need for them to set up a legally separate subsidiary in each EU country, on the basis of different national legislations, in which they wish to operate.

It is too early to assess the impact of the opening-up of the market in insurance services. Some firms say they notice little difference. In one survey, however, a British company said it switched its insurance business to France where two groups had offered lower rates than its previous British insurer.

In the area of telecommunications services, liberalization is forging ahead. The EU has long recognized the importance of a deregulated and competitive telecommunications sector both in its own right and as part of the essential infrastructure of a modern economy. High-quality and efficient telecommunications services are essential working tools for many other sectors of the economy from banking and manufacturing to transport.

EKA

Motorists can take out car insurance with firms in other Member States if better terms are available there.

Can you open a bank account or borrow money in another country?

Since 1 January 1993, anyone living in the European Union has been entitled to carry out unrestricted capital operations within the Union.

For administrative or statistical purposes, the Member States are allowed to impose procedures for the declaration of capital movements and to take such measures as may be required to prevent their laws and regulations from being broken. But the means used may in no circumstances serve to prevent movements of capital.

Example: a Member State may not oblige a citizen suspected of using a foreign account to avoid paying tax on interest, to close that account and repatriate the capital. All it can do is require the citizen to declare the interest credited to the account.

Although several Member States encountered early problems in transposing directives liberalizing some telecommunications services, the pace of deregulation elsewhere is speeding up. Competition among telecommunications operators for basic voice telephony (which still accounts for more than 80% of the entire telecommunications sector) is now set for January 1998 with liberalization of the network infrastructure scheduled to take place at the same time.

Like telecommunications, transport is a vital sector of the EU economy, representing more than 7% of gross domestic product (GDP). Transport services are also being progressively liberalized even if the January 1993 deadline was not fully respected. On that date quota restrictions on hauliers imposed by other EU governments were finally lifted.

But a regulation enabling road transport companies to bid for domestic business in other EU countries was only adopted in October 1993. This brings road transport up to the level of liberalization already reached in the air and maritime sectors.

The fourth freedom

The freedom of movement of capital was the first of the four fundamental freedoms of the single market to be realized. The basic directive removing all capital controls was adopted in 1988. This has been followed by a series of directives liberalizing banking and financial services. One essential element which remains to be put in place is a directive on how savings should be taxed, which remains blocked because of differences between Member States.

The strategic programme: Making the most of the internal market

Faced with the task of completing, managing and developing the single market programme, the European Commission published its strategic programme in December 1993. This is a guide to the main priorities of the single market for the coming years and a means of measuring its progress towards meeting its objectives.

As the Commission itself notes: 'The establishment of a genuine single market is not just a matter of adopting Community-level legislation within a deadline. It is a continual process of ensuring that the common legal framework is applied, widely understood, enforced and, where necessary, developed in a coherent way to meet new needs. In that sense, the Union is at the beginning, not at the end, of its task'.

The strategic programme, *inter alia*, draws important links between the single market and other Union policies. It stresses the important contribution to ensuring the effective operation of the single market made by competition policy, consumer policy and policy in favour of SMEs.

Competition policy must make sure that the four freedoms established by the single market are not eroded by State subsidies to companies, anti-competitive agreements and mergers or the abuse of dominant positions by large enterprises. It also has a role to play in opening the single market to areas not covered by the original 1985 liberalization programme.

EKA

A European Union directive prohibits unfair terms in consumer contracts. After-sales service and access to justice are secured so as to protect the consumer against the risks of a market offering a wide range of highly sophisticated products.

Consumer policy protects the interests of consumers and empowers them to make sure the single market works in ways which permit them to draw a maximum benefit from the removal of obstacles to free trade and free movement. SME policy should be geared to making sure that these firms can take advantage of the opportunities and respond to the challenges presented by the single market.

Savings thanks to the single market

The disappearance of the European Union's internal frontiers has resulted in administrative savings to Dutch firms amounting to HFL 538 million a year. The only new expenditure firms are having to meet — HFL 105 million — relates to the adaptation of administrative procedures, the management of statistics and the training of employees in the new administrative procedures.

These figures are taken from surveys conducted by the Dutch Ministry of Economic Affairs.

This reduction in costs is mainly attributable to the abolition of customs forms.

Consumer protection

Nowadays, producers and distributors are only permitted to market products which they guarantee as safe. This applies not only to mass-produced goods but also to specific products, such as dangerous substances. Very precise rules require product labels to state the nature of the risk and provide guidance on handling. For example, seven symbols used on mass-produced products (washing powders, solvents, paints, etc.) convey an immediate visual message (explosive, flammable, corrosive, etc.).

Downstream from this EU framework, responsibility for product surveillance lies with the national authorities, who make daily inspections at production and distribution facilities. If, however, a dangerous product were to slip through the net, its progress should be halted by an EU information-exchange and rapid alert system. A Member State which withdraws a product presenting an immediate danger to the consumer from the market, whether a food product or not, has to notify the European Commission, which then alerts the other Member States within a few hours, thus enabling them to take appropriate measures immediately.

Safeguarding the cultural heritage

Originally, Article 36 of the Treaty of Rome stipulated that the Member States could prohibit or restrict exports of 'national treasures possessing artistic, historic or archaeological value'. This right has not been removed by the arrival of the single market and the abolition of customs checks at the internal borders does not deprive works of art of effective protection, which is now organized at Community level.

Since 1993, for example, prior authorization may be required before some categories of such goods may leave the European Union (Regulation (EEC) No 394/92 of 9 December 1992).

This authorization, which is issued by the customs services of the country where the cultural asset is lawfully located, is valid in all Union States.

Furthermore, cultural goods which are unlawfully located in a Member State of the Union must be returned to the Member State of origin subject to certain conditions (Directive 93/7/EEC of 15 March 1993).

Completing the single market

Although the removal of identity checks at frontiers is the biggest item of unfinished single market business, other parts of the original project still need to be put in place. Incomplete legislation in the area of company law is a continuing obstacle to the mobility of firms within the single market.

In this sector, agreement is still needed among Member States on the draft statute for a European company as well as on arrangements to avoid double taxation of company revenues. As for taxation, VAT provisions still need to be harmonized on second-hand goods, works of art, antiques and collectors' items, gold transactions and passenger transport.

Harmonized rules for intellectual and industrial property make an important contribution to the effective functioning of the single market. Here a number of directives still await adoption. These include a directive on the protection of personal data which the European Commission considers a priority in view of the increase in the flow of personal data in the private and public sectors that is resulting from the removal of internal frontiers within the EU.

EKA

Copyright and related rights are to enjoy better protection in the single market. Harmonization is in progress to protect creativity in Europe.

As part of its task of completing the single market, the EU is introducing competition into certain sectors such as telecommunications, postal services, energy distribution and air transport where national monopolies have been operating in most Member States. The aim is to promote intra-Union competition while taking account of public and consumer interests such as the supply of a universal service for telecommunications and postal services to subscribers throughout the Member States at fair prices, irrespective of geographic location.

The liberalization of telecommunications services is well under way, but progress has been slower in the postal sector. EU governments have moved more slowly towards consensus on postal services, partly because of the key role postal services play particularly in rural communities throughout the European Union.

In the field of air transport, the Commission has prepared a proposal for the liberalization of ground handling facilities at EU airports.

Managing the single market

The bulk of the single market legislative package has taken the form of directives. These are adopted at EU level and set the requirements and objectives which Member States must respect. But Member States have considerable liberty in the way they transpose the directives into national legal instruments and how they actually meet the requirements of each directive.

The need to ensure that directives are being transposed correctly and enforced in the right way is the biggest challenge facing those responsible for managing the single market. Incorrect or incomplete transposition, or the lack of transposition altogether, and inadequate enforcement procedures can allow differences to emerge in the way individual governments actually implement each directive. This in turn can create new obstacles to the flow of goods and services between Member States — exactly the opposite of what the single market sets out to achieve.

Ensuring the effective transposition of directives into national law is, of course, primarily the task of individual governments. But the European Commission has the responsibility for ensuring that Member States fulfil their obligations under EU law. It must therefore monitor transposition measures to verify that they are adopted and that they correspond to the requirements of the directives.

Dialogue

The European Union has set up the facilities it needs to encourage cooperation in the operation of the single market. Any problems that arise are dealt with by an advisory committee of senior civil servants.

There is also a committee that listens to the business world's needs so that dialogue there can make the single market function better.

How the Commission keeps check

The Commission uses a combination of methods to ensure that governments transpose and implement single market directives correctly:

Comprehensive monitoring of texts: this is a time-consuming task. Commission staff can carry it out in sectors where only a relatively small body of law is involved. In some other areas, the Commission has to rely on outside consultants to carry out the work on its behalf. This approach has limitations.

Contacts with Member States: multilateral or bilateral meetings (depending on the nature of the issue) can assist in interpreting directives and in identifying potential areas of difficulty.

Direct contacts with economic operators: the various networks via which the Commission maintains contact with economic operators (business representatives, professional associations, etc.) are a useful source of information on problems with transposition measures.

Complaints procedures: individuals and businesses can draw the Commission's attention to problems they encounter with Member States' legislation. This approach depends on complainants being aware of their rights under EU law.

EKA

In the complex work of transposing and enforcing directives clearly a partnership between the Commission and member governments is necessary. The partnership needs to cover the whole range of relevant policy areas. The single market is like other aspects of the European Union: if it stops advancing, it regresses. Cooperation needs to be reinforced by specific measures such as the development of a communications and data-exchange network among national administrations and between them and the Commission.

In the single market the authorities of the Member States and the Community have to administer the same set of common rules. The European Commission now has long-standing experience but even so it works with the national authorities on ways of improving and streamlining administrative cooperation.
This cooperation will have to be kept under regular review if it is to keep in step with the needs of the Union's citizens and firms.

EKA

The European Union has its own body of animal health legislation; it applies to animals to be shipped from one Member State to another.

In the case of infringements of EU law by Member States, the Commission can take action against them and open proceedings before the European Court of Justice. These powers have been strengthened under the Maastricht Treaty which gives the Court the right to impose financial penalties on governments which fail to comply with its rulings.

Throughout the process of monitoring and enforcing the application of EU directives, lines of communication between national governments and the Commission have to be kept open to make sure a maximum number of problems are solved without recourse to the Court.

Enforcement of EU directives must be of high quality to prevent new trade barriers being created, inadvertently or deliberately, by Member States. Governments should examine whether intended national legislation may put at risk any of the four fundamental freedoms of the single market.

Under the single market, individuals and companies resident in one Member State will increasingly need to claim their rights in another. Procedures for redress and access to justice via national courts and the European Court of Justice are therefore important.

They need to be simplified, made more transparent and explained to a wider audience. Doubts about the fairness of EU justice or about obtaining redress can represent a significant obstacle to cross-border transactions and therefore to the proper functioning of the single market.

The next step: Developing the single market

As the dynamics of the single market push forward, new issues will emerge and new needs will have to be taken care of that were not foreseen by planners. This is already happening as the Commission's contacts with market operators have clearly shown.

The response from the market was unequivocal: there is much unfinished work to attend to. Representatives from business and industry strongly supported continued harmonization of legislation in a limited number of fields such as direct taxation and the protection of intellectual property. They have also pushed for it in sectors like foodstuffs, electronics, electrical components, chemicals and pharmaceuticals.

SMEs pressed for greater opportunities to enable them to participate in the single market. Consumer organizations, while welcoming the single market's commitment to defend consumer interests, called for a more ambitious approach.

A large number of those consulted, including the European Parliament and national governments, insisted on the role of competition policy in upholding the principles of the single market. Others raised the issue of ensuring compatibility between the management of the single market and the EU's commitment to sustainable development and the protection of the environment.

Framework programmes for research

The European countries spend less on research than their competitors — 2% of GDP for the Union, as against 2.8% for the USA and 3% for Japan.

To overcome this handicap, aggravated as it is by the fragmented nature of resources and the duplication of efforts between national programmes, the Union has set up framework programmes, mainly for the benefit of information/communication technologies, advanced materials, the environment and life and energy technologies.

The basic instrument of this policy is cooperation between enterprises, laboratories and universities of different countries on joint projects subsidized at a rate of 50% by the European Commission.

The Union also takes part in a number of projects going beyond the borders. A major example of this is Eureka, which focuses on the design of new products which can be placed rapidly on the market.

Can a Member State apply an autonomous competition policy in the single market?

In the single market, all firms in all the Member States are entitled to sell their products, purchase the goods and services they require and extend their activities by direct investment in other Member States.

Powers are distributed between the Union itself and the Member States in such a way that the Union takes charge of those matters which can best be dealt with at that level while the Member States exercise their national powers in those, far more numerous, cases where satisfactory solutions can best be arrived at in that way.

The 1989 merger control Regulation is a good example: it distinguishes between major operations with a Community dimension, which are scrutinized by the Commission, and cases with more of a national impact, which fall within the terms of reference of the Member States. The principle of this distribution is not actually confined to mergers but concerns the entire policy on business competition.

As for consumers, they are spending more and more on products from other Member States, resulting in a greater range of available products and fewer opportunities for firms to exploit large price differences between countries. Competition is thus making itself felt increasingly across the borders.

In the single market firms in all Union Member States are now allowed to tender for public works throughout the Union. This is a tricky area, traditionally reserved for national firms. There have been serious delays in attaining the objectives of the single market.

EKA

In all areas of activity, people throughout the Union need more information about single market laws and how they apply. They require assurance that new laws will only be introduced where they are essential for the functioning of the single market.

Support for SMEs

Small and medium-sized enterprises form the backbone of the European economy. They account for 99% of registered companies and provide more than 70% of private-sector jobs. SMEs themselves vary enormously in size, structure and scope and type of activity. But they share many common problems which limit their ability to participate fully in the advantages of the single market.

A number of action lines are being prepared. One is to increase their access to finance. Many SMEs are undercapitalized and often cannot raise funds for investment or marketing because of their inability to provide collateral. New operational mechanisms to limit this handicap are needed.

A second priority is to help SMEs adapt to standardization and quality assurance procedures. All SMEs should have access to detailed information on existing and draft European standards. Their interests should be taken on board in the process of writing new standards.

A third need is to open up public procurement markets to SMEs. They often find it difficult to compete effectively for contracts because of the onerous administrative requirements linked to submitting a tender bid. The lack of a local partner in the country where the contract is being awarded is another handicap.

The idea is to facilitate the creation of cross-border partnerships via EU networks like BC-Net and the BRE 'marriage bureau'. Advice available to them from private and public bodies should also be improved as should access to TED, the Commission's electronic information system on public tenders across the Union.

Trans-European networks (TENs)

Trans-European networks (TENs) are destined to become the arteries along which the economic lifeblood of the European Union flows. People, goods and services must be able to move around the market efficiently and at the lowest possible cost. The networks in question consist of large cross-border projects in the sectors of communications, transport and energy distribution.

At present the economic infrastructures of the individual countries of the Union are inward-looking, often with the national capital city as their nerve centre. The aim of the TEN programme is to take the single market as the starting point and create continent-wide networks which are planned and set up according to the logic of a single economy. In this way, TENs become instruments of economic integration, facilitating communications, shrinking distances and bringing outlying and peripheral areas into easier contact with central regions.

Although central to the functioning of the single market, TENs are also vital for the attainment of a number of other Union goals such as:

• the reinforcement of social and economic cohesion between the rich and poorer areas of the EU. Efficient communications, both transport and electronic, bind the peripheral areas of the Union more closely to the centre. Since these areas have per capita incomes well below the EU average, TENs should help accelerate economic development and promote convergence with other national economies;

• the setting of infrastructure priorities. The same outlying areas suffer from a lack of infrastructure, both in terms of quantity and quality, which can be remedied by an active Union policy;

• the strengthening of economic competitiveness. Their absence results in lost opportunities to create new markets and leaves the EU with a level of job creation that falls short of its real potential;

• the creation of links between the countries of the Union and their neighbours in Eastern Europe and the Mediterranean.

Political impetus at the highest level

In view of their importance, the accelerated achievement of TENs was itself given the status of a priority Union policy by EU Heads of State or Government at their Brussels Summit in December 1993. TENs also figure prominently in the Commission's White Paper on growth, competitiveness and employment, endorsed by the Brussels Summit as a blueprint for post-recession economic recovery.

The aim of Union action is to reduce the financial and administrative risks involved in the development of multi-billion ecu cross-border projects and to get private investors to take a greater share in their financing. In essence, this means fostering partnerships between all concerned: public authorities, network operators, service providers, users, financiers and industrialists.

In all three network categories, projects of common European interest are identified as having a special priority. These will qualify, among other things, for financial support from the EU in the preparation of feasibility studies as well as for loan guarantees and interest rate subsidies.

List of priority transport projects

Work begun or to begin by the end of 1996

1.	High-speed train / Combined transport north-south Nürnberg-Erfurt-Halle/Leipzig-Berlin Brenner axis: Verona-München	I/A/D
2.	High-speed train (Paris)-Brussels-Köln-Amsterdam-London	
	Belgium: border-Brussels-Liège-B/D border; Brussels-B/NL border	B
	United Kingdom: London-Channel Tunnel access	UK
	Netherlands: B/NL border-Rotterdam-Amsterdam	NL
	Germany: (Aachen[1]) Köln-Rhein/Main	D
3.	High-speed train south Madrid-Barcelona-Perpignan-Montpellier Madrid-Vitoria-Dax	E/F
4.	High-speed train east	
	Paris-Metz-Strasbourg-Appenweier-(Karlsruhe)	F/D
	with junctions to Metz-Saarbrücken-Mannheim	F/D
	and Metz-Luxembourg	F/L
5.	Conventional rail/combined transport: Betuwe line Rotterdam-NL/D border-(Rhein/Ruhr[1])	NL/D
6.	High-speed train/combined transport France-Italy Lyon-Torino; Torino-Milano-Venezia-Trieste	F/I
7.	Greek motorways: Pathe: Rio Antirio, Patras-Athens-Thessaloniki-Prohamon (Greek/Bulgarian border) and Via Egnatia: Igoumenitsa-Thessaloniki-Alexandroupolis-Ormenio (Greek/Bulgarian border)-Kipi (Greek-Turkish border)	GR
8.	Motorway Lisbon-Valladolid	P/E
9.	Conventional rail link Cork-Dublin-Belfast-Larne-Stranraer	IRL/UK
10.	Malpensa airport (Milano)	I
11.	Fixed rail/road link between Denmark and Sweden (Øresund fixed link) including access routes for road, rail, air	DK/S
12.	Nordic Triangle (rail/road)	FIN/S
13.	Ireland/United Kingdom/Benelux road link	UK/(IRL)
14.	West coast main line (rail)	UK

---

[1] Ongoing construction — support already provided at Community level.

Choosing priorities

At its 1994 meetings (Corfu in June and Essen in December), the European Council adopted a list of 14 priority transport projects and called on Member States concerned to do everything necessary to advance these projects and to accelerate administrative, statutory and legislative procedures. Work on these projects will begin by the end of 1996 at the latest. Some are already under way.

The priority projects include the development of high-speed train networks to provide fast, safe and environment-friendly links between the principal population centres of the Union. The network consists of 23 000 kilometres of track, of which 10 000 will be new lines for speeds in excess of 250 km/h. Several of the lines will be for both passenger and freight services, including combined road/rail transport.

One of the principal concerns of TENs in the rail sector, but also in other sectors, will be to ensure that the different parts of the network are compatible with each other and that trains are interoperable, that is, they can easily move from one part of the network to another.

The present limited high-speed service linking Paris, London and Brussels requires locomotives to have triple systems for converting electric power because national standards differ in each country. Moreover, there are no overhead electricity cables for trains in south-east England and while on the British side of the Channel Tunnel, high-speed trains from Paris or Brussels must pick up electricity from the third rail system on the track.

In the energy sector, the main TEN priority is to interconnect national electricity grids and gas pipelines within and between Member States as well as with neighbouring countries. For gas, special attention will be given to developing new supply lines from gas fields in Russia, Central Asia and North Africa.

In the telecommunications sector, the best example of an integrated European network is that of the GSM system for digital mobile telephone communications. This system, created in 1989, was a TEN before its time. It is now operating in virtually every Union country. GSM is also a success story for European technology and is poised to become the world standard for digital mobile telephony.

The main thrust of the agreed policy on information highways is that the process of liberalization, including the ending of monopolies on network infrastructures, should be accelerated. In the meantime, the integrated services digital network (ISDN) is being developed as the basic European public telecommunications network. ISDN is a multipurpose general network which already exists in six EU countries. Via a single access point, it can offer a wide range of services for the transmission of voice, data and image.

The external dimension of the single market

It would defeat the purpose of trans-European networks to stop at the Union's borders. The completion of the single market must also be linked to establishing closer relations with the Union's neighbours. The EU is committed to extending networks to its neighbours in Central and Eastern Europe.

At their meeting in Copenhagen in June 1993, Heads of State or Government agreed that a maximum of 15% of the funding of the PHARE programme of technical assistance to Central and Eastern Europe could go on infrastructure projects, principally TENs.

The EU's contribution will underpin the vocation of Central and East European countries to become Union members.

The Commission produced a White Paper by June 1995, setting out a strategy for assisting the Central and East European countries to prepare themselves for integration with the single market after accession.

Is the single market accessible?

The EU accounts for 38% of world trade as opposed to 11% for the United States and 9% for Japan. Its economic well-being thus depends on its imports and exports. It is therefore very open to all States wishing to trade with it.

Access to the Community market is based on negotiated terms.

GATT (General Agreement on Tariffs and Trade) and its successor, the World Trade Organization (WTO) set up mechanisms for the management of free trade between the various contracting parties. In negotiations with the United States and Japan, the Union has systematically striven to remove barriers to trade.

Outside the fields covered by GATT and WTO, the Union negotiates terms for the access of goods and services from non-member countries to its market. For example, until 1987, there was no redress available against firms in the United States who, by copying European microcircuits, caused enormous damage to the European car, telecommunications and medical equipment industries. In 1987, the Union introduced a uniform system for the protection of microcircuits, thereby shielding its products from American copies.

Global responsibilities

The creation of the single market reinforces the Union's importance as the world's leading trading power. It gives the EU a more solid internal base to help carry out its international responsibilities and to defend its legitimate trading interests. It has stated its intention to do so vigorously within the framework of trade policy instruments available under the new World Trade Organization (WTO), successor to the General Agreement on Tariffs and Trade (GATT).

EU trade policy has long been implemented at Union level via the common commercial policy rather than by Member States. As a result, it has concluded trade agreements with most countries and regional groupings around the world. This also explains why the EU as such was able to play such a leading role in the Uruguay Round of multilateral trade liberalization negotiations which were formally concluded in March 1994.

EKA

Quality goods are what the single market is there to produce. Standardization is not enough; competitiveness is what is really needed.

Thanks to the common commercial policy, the benefits of the single market are available to firms from outside the EU on the same terms as their European rivals. The single market is open to everyone on a strictly competitive basis.

Contrary to earlier fears expressed by some trading partners, the Union has not created the single market as an inward-looking 'fortress Europe'. Once inside Union territory, imported goods move as freely across internal EU frontiers as local products. This means they too need to conform to only one set of national or EU standards to have access to the national markets of all Member States, instead of adopting one standard per country as was previously the case.

In a few areas like financial services and public procurement, the EU has introduced a proviso whereby foreign firms have full access to the EU market as long as European companies have similar open access to their home markets. This is the so-called reciprocity requirement.

The EU is ready to negotiate mutual market access agreements with governments who want entry to the European market for their firms either multilaterally or on a bilateral basis. In this way, the single market is enabling European firms to enter foreign markets as it extends its own advantages to non-EU companies.

A dynamic commercial policy must be accompanied by the efficient management of the Union's external frontiers if individuals and firms, both European and non-EU alike, are to reap the full benefits of the single market. Action is needed in the general interest to curb illicit practices or trade distortions that could undermine the competitive functioning of Union markets.

Close cooperation between national administrations and the European Commission is needed to prevent infringements of customs rules and other conditions of access to the EU market. Priority areas include fraud prevention, the protection of intellectual property rights — trade marks, designs and copyright — and measures to combat counterfeiting.

A balance needs to be struck between deterring and detecting evasion and malpractice on the one hand, and the need to ensure minimum disruption to legitimate trade and free movement on the other.

Above all, customs services at all external frontiers throughout the EU must be trained to the same high standards of efficiency. They must apply their skills with the same uniform degrees of quality. Only in this way will the necessary confidence be built up in the single market. With the disappearance of national customs controls at internal frontiers, officials and citizens of one country must feel confident that goods or persons arriving on their territory via an EU neighbour have passed the same level of controls their own customs service would have applied.

The single market and new policies

The Maastricht Treaty extended the responsibility of the Union in policy areas like the environment, education and training, health and cultural matters. At the same time, the EU has accepted international commitments in areas like environmental protection and sustainable development. The single market must take account of these changes.

Sustainable development

There is no inherent conflict between the consolidation of the single market and the fight against environmental degradation; the two are mutually supportive. The Single European Act of 1987 already stated that the completion of the single market is an important means of achieving *inter alia* a sustainable and non-inflationary growth which respects the environment.

Previous ideas of short-term economic gains being possible at the expense of the environment are being replaced by an attitude where competitiveness and efficiency form the basis for a more sustainable long-term economic pattern, both within the EU and internationally.

EKA

In recent years there has been a new tendency to seek sustainable, harmonious economic growth that respects the environment as a priority consideration.

But a great information effort will still have to be made to secure general acceptance of the principle and give effect to it everywhere; there are still threats to the environment, notably from waste.

EKA

Does the single market encourage the free movement of waste?

Waste is also a commercial commodity. However, to prevent abuses in the fields of transport and storage, the transfer of waste from one Member State to another is subject to special rules.

These special rules are warranted by the magnitude and environmental impact of the waste problem. Two billion tonnes of waste are produced in the European Union every year, of which 20 to 30 million tonnes are dangerous. Dangerous and/or toxic waste needs to be treated by the best available methods and technology to ensure a high level of protection for the environment and public health.

Since waste cannot always be treated or recycled safely enough at the place of production, it may have to cross an internal border for storage, treatment, reconditioning or recycling. Paradoxically, therefore, the free movement of waste acts as a safeguard against unauthorized dumping.

Under the EU's fifth environment action plan, an integrated approach is being developed to make sure that the most effective policy is applied in seeking a more sustainable path to economic and social development. This is vital not only for the environment but for the long-term success of the single market itself. Its viability depends on the sustainability of the policies pursued in the field of industry, energy, transport, agriculture and tourism, which are in turn dependent on the capacity of the environment to sustain them.

Many environmental issues like climate change, acid rain and waste management have cross-border ramifications and can only be tackled through cooperation among economic operators and sectors and through a mix of policy instruments. These aims can best be achieved within the single market context.

Acid rain in one country can result from sulphur emissions by industrial plants located in another. The quality of Dutch drinking water drawn from the Rhine depends on substances which enter the river upstream of Dutch territory.

The EU has already acted in a number of sectors, for instance by limiting the toxic content of automobile exhausts, lowering permitted pollution levels from municipal incinerators, and restricting transborder shipments of hazardous waste.

In some landmark decisions, the European Court of Justice has ruled that environmental considerations can, in certain circumstances, be more important than free trade principles. At the international level, the EU supports efforts to create an international framework for resolving trade conflicts arising from the application of national or regional measures designed to protect the environment.

The EU has joined international agreements to eliminate by 1995 the use of chemicals, known as CFCs (chlorofluorocarbons), which deplete the earth's protective ozone layer. The Union also accepted a moral commitment at the 1992 Earth Summit in Rio de Janeiro to stabilize emissions of carbon dioxide (CO_2) — the presumed main cause of global warming — by the year 2000.

Education and health

The accelerating pace of technological change and the consolidation of the single market call for greater adaptability and mobility of the workforce in EC countries. The EU Member States have recognized education as a priority sector because it will provide the skilled workers needed as the European economy enters the 21st century. Education is one key to reducing unemployment, particularly among young people. This is why the EU will reinforce earlier actions such as the funding of vocational training measures through the European Social Fund.

The European Union already does a great deal to protect the health of its citizens. By the year 2000, the Europe against cancer programme, which promotes cooperation between researchers as well as education and preventive measures, should reduce the number of cancer deaths by 15%. Under the Maastricht Treaty, the Union is able to support cooperation between Member States in disease prevention efforts, particularly as concerns AIDS and drug dependence.

EKA

A large set of veterinary rules has been established for the European Union, making it possible to abolish frontier health checks. But checks at the Union's external frontiers have been boosted and harmonized as between Member States. This took a long time to achieve, and the rate of progress was by no means the same in all Member States. But the experts' view is that the last two years have been good years in this respect.

What about health?

To safeguard public health in the European Union, foodstuffs have to undergo scientific analysis. The Union has a Scientific Committee for Food, a Scientific Veterinary Committee and a Scientific Committee for Pesticides to oversee these matters.

The Scientific Committee for Food, which consists of a number of eminent experts in medicine, nutrition, toxicology, biology, chemistry, etc., affords the Commission scientific support which is particularly important given the primordial need to protect public health.

In addition to delivering opinions on matters referred to it by the Commission, the Committee may draw its attention to any aspect of food consumption which has implications for health. In such cases, it gives its views on the composition of foodstuffs and the various methods by which they are treated and also on the presence of additives and contaminants.

This work is very important to the drafting of Community legislation.

From single market to single currency

Economic and monetary union (EMU) and the creation of a single currency are the essential follow-up to the creation of the single market so that it can function efficiently. Businessmen and industrialists throughout Europe support its introduction, even if some EU governments, like the British and Danish, have not yet committed themselves to the final stage of the process.

It was, in fact, the dynamism generated by the success of the single market programme that inspired the European Community (as it still was) to extend integration into the critical but sensitive areas of EMU and political union. The notion of creating a single currency, the euro, is a logical extension of the single market: with the removal of other barriers, the transaction costs of transferring funds from one currency to another become a major cost item.

The process of economic and monetary union has already started. In June 1989, Heads of State or Government decided that with the recent abolition of capital controls and given the smooth functioning of the European Monetary System and the exchange-rate mechanism (ERM) which linked member currencies within narrow fluctuation margins, the first stage of EMU would begin on 1 July 1990. It duly did.

Bank transfers in the EU – Too expensive and too slow

To transfer money from one Member State to another, businesses and individuals now have to pay an average of ECU 2.54 per ECU 100 transferred. According to a survey carried out by the European Commission, this represents an increase of ECU 2 on a year ago. The average time required to carry out a transfer order is five working days while in the individual Member States the time may range from three to eight working days.

For its survey, the Commission used a sample consisting of 352 bank branches, which it requested to process 1 000 urgent and 100 non-urgent bank transfers. Non-urgent transfer orders tended to cost less but, surprisingly, they were also processed more quickly.

Orders take longest to process in Portugal, Ireland and Greece. According to the survey, it is British banks which charge the highest for transfers but, at the same time, they are also the banks which process orders in the shortest time. Overall costs are highest in France, the United Kingdom and Greece and lowest in Italy, the Netherlands and Luxembourg.

Phase two also began on schedule on 1 January 1994 despite the currency crises of 1992 and 1993 and the deep economic recession which had blown EU currencies and national economies off course.

But in fact the first two phases of EMU do not include far-reaching innovations in the area of economic policy or currency management. The big changes come with the third and final phase.

At the start of phase two, as required under the Treaty on European Union, EU governments set up the European Monetary Institute (EMI), precursor of the European Central Bank (ECB). They also committed themselves to intensive preparations for phase three. Countries whose inflation rates and government debt are too high must adopt policies aimed at bringing them down to the levels of the more stable EU economies. All governments are committed in stage two to avoid excessive deficits in their national budgets.

Because of the recession and the 1992/93 currency turbulence, the Union could not implement the first option in the Maastricht Treaty to move to stage three of EMU on 1 January 1997. To meet this deadline, a majority of EU members were required to respect the strict economic and fiscal criteria set for EMU membership. This was not the case.

However, EU leaders confirmed at the Madrid European Council in December 1995 the second option contained in the Treaty. This is that the final stage of EMU will begin on 1 January 1999 even if only a minority of Member States qualify to join. Operations in the single currency, the euro, will begin on the same date.

The entry ticket

The final decision as to which countries will qualify for stage three will be taken as soon as possible in 1998. The criteria Member States must meet to qualify for EMU are tough ones. They are contained in the Maastricht Treaty on European Union and concern price stability, public finances, exchange rates and interest rates.

Price stability: qualifying countries must show that their inflation over the last year preceding the start of phase three was within $1\frac{1}{2}$ percentage points of the three EU countries with the lowest rates of inflation.

Public finances: they must also demonstrate that their budget deficits are no more than 3% of GDP and that their outstanding government debt is less than 60% of GDP.

Exchange rates: they must not have devalued their currency in the two years prior to phase three and must have kept their currency within normal ERM margins during this period.

Interest rates: qualifying countries must also have average nominal long-term interest rates that are within 2 percentage points of the three EU States with the lowest rates.

The single currency

Although the introduction of a single currency will start in 1999, the process will be phased over three and a half years. On 1 January 1999, the currencies of those countries entering stage three will be irrevocably locked together. The euro will then be introduced for official payments, extending gradually to cover commercial operations and electronic banking payments and transfers. Euro notes and coins will be brought in between January and June 2002, completing the full introduction of the single currency.

The euro will replace the present ecu, which can be considered as the forerunner of the single currency. Ecus will be converted into euros on a one-for-one basis.

The ecu has, in fact, existed for a number of years. But its use has been limited. The French and Belgian Governments have issued ecu coins, but they are collectors' items of symbolic importance. Its main function has been in international finance, although ordinary citizens can use it for non-cash transactions like cheques or bank transfers or deposits in savings accounts.

The ecu is principally used for loan issues on the international capital market by EU institutions, governments and multinational corporations. Some large corporations use the ecu for accounting purposes. It also serves for mutual settlements between EU central banks.

A wider context

The single market is not just a step on the way towards full economic and monetary union. It must also serve as the anchor for the Union as it prepares for the two other challenges it faces between now and the year 2000.

One is the Intergovernmental Conference (IGC) to take place in 1996 to review and update the Treaty on European Union. Wide-ranging institutional reforms, the extension of the Treaty to cover defence issues and the reinforcement of the EU's democratic structures are all on the agenda.

The second challenge is the next enlargement. Negotiations to bring in Central and East European countries will follow the completion of the IGC. By early in the next century, the single market may have to cope with 20 or more member countries.

European Commission

THE SINGLE MARKET

Luxembourg: Office for Official Publications of the European Communities

1996 – 44 pp. – 16.2 x 22.9 cm

ISBN 92-827-7822-3

Since 1993, 370 million European citizens and thousands of companies have benefited from the European single market.
The booklet gives information about this market and its workings.

European Commission

Rue de la Loi 200, B-1049 Bruxelles

BELGIQUE/BELGIË

Rue Archimède 73
B-1000 BRUXELLES
Archimedesstraat 73
B-1000 BRUSSEL
Tél. (32-2) 295 38 44
Fax (32-2) 295 01 66

DANMARK

Højbrohus
Østergade 61
Postbox 144
DK-1004 KØBENHAVN K
Tlf. (45) 33 14 41 40
Fax (45) 33 11 12 03/14 13 92 (sekretariat)
(45) 33 14 14 47 (dokumentation)

DEUTSCHLAND

Zitelmannstraße 22
D-53113 BONN
Postfach 53106 BONN
Tel. (49-228) 53 00 90
Fernkopie (49-228) 53 00 950/12

Kurfürstendamm 102
D-10711 BERLIN
Tel. (49-30) 896 09 30
Fernkopie (49-30) 892 20 59

Erhardtstraße 27
D-80331 MÜNCHEN
Tel. (49-89) 202 10 11
Fernschreiber (041) 52 18 135
Fernkopie (49-89) 202 10 15

GREECE/ΕΛΛΑΔΑ

Vassilissis Sofias 2
T.K. 30 284
GR-106 74 ATHINA
Tel. (30-1) 725 10 00
Telefax (30-1) 724 46 20

ESPAÑA

Paseo de la Castellana, 46
E-28046 MADRID
Tel. (34-1) 431 57 11
Fax (34-1) 576 03 87/577 29 23

Av. Diagonal, 407 bis, 18ª
E-08008 BARCELONA
Tel. (34-3) 415 81 77 (5 líneas)
Fax (34-3) 415 63 11

FRANCE

288, boulevard Saint-Germain
F-75007 PARIS
Pour obtenir les publications:
Centre d'information et de documentation
«Sources d'Europe»
Socle de la Grande Arche
F-92054 Paris La Défense Cedex 61
Tél. (33-1) 41 25 12 12

CMCI
2, rue Henri Barbusse
F-13241 MARSEILLE Cedex 01
Tél. (33) 91 91 46 00
Fax (33) 91 90 98 07

IRELAND

Jean Monnet Centre
18 Dawson Street
DUBLIN 2
Tel. (353-1) 662 51 13
Fax (353-1) 662 51 18

ITALIA

Via Poli, 29
I-00187 ROMA
Tel. (39-6) 699 991
Telecopia (39-6) 679 16 58/679 36 52

Corso Magenta, 59
I-20123 MILANO
Tel. (39-2) 48 01 25 05
Telecopia (39-2) 481 85 43

LUXEMBOURG

Bâtiment Jean Monnet
Rue Alcide De Gasperi
L-2920 LUXEMBOURG
Tél. (352) 43 01-34925
Fax (352) 43 01-34433

NEDERLAND

Korte Vijverberg 5
NL-2513 AB DEN HAAG
Postbus 30465
NL-2500 GL DEN HAAG
Tel. (31-70) 346 93 26
Telefax (31-70) 364 66 19

ÖSTERREICH

Hoyosgasse 5
A-1040 WIEN
Tel. (43-1) 505 33 79
Fax (43-1) 505 33 797

PORTUGAL

Centro Europeu Jean Monnet
Largo Jean Monnet, 1-10.º
P-1200 LISBOA
Tel. (351-1) 350 98 00
Telecópia (351-1) 355 43 97/
/350 98 01/350 98 02/350 98 03

SUOMI/FINLAND

Pohjoisesplanadi 31
PL 234
FIN-00131 HELSINKI
Norra esplanaden 31
PB 234
FIN-00131 HELSINGFORS
Puh. (358-0) 65 64 20
Fax (358-0) 65 67 28

SVERIGE

Box 7323
Hamngatan 6
S-103 90 STOCKHOLM
Tel. (46-8) 611 11 72
Fax (46-8) 611 44 35

UNITED KINGDOM

Jean Monnet House
8 Storey's Gate
LONDON SW1P 3AT
Tel. (44-71) 973 19 92
Fax (44-71) 973 19 00/19 10/18 95

Windsor House
9/15 Bedford Street
BELFAST BT2 7EG
Tel. (44-232) 24 07 08
Fax (44-232) 24 82 41

4 Cathedral Road
CARDIFF CF1 9SG
Tel. (44-222) 37 16 31
Fax (44-222) 39 54 89

9 Alva Street
EDINBURGH EH2 4PH
Tel. (44-31) 225 20 58
Fax (44-31) 226 41 05

UNITED STATES OF AMERICA

2300 M Street, NW
WASHINGTON, DC 20037
Tel. (202) 862 95 00
Fax (202) 429 17 66

3 Dag Hammarskjöld Plaza
305 East 47th Street
NEW YORK, NY 10017
Tel. (212) 371 38 04
Fax (212) 758 27 18/688 10 13

NIPPON

Europa House
9-15 Sanbancho
Chiyoda-Ku
TOKYO 102
Tel. (813) 239 04 41
Fax (813) 32 39 93 37/32 61 51 94